WEEKLY WR READER®
EARLY LEARNING LIBRARY

Things with Wings

THE LIFE CYCLE OF A
DRAGONFLY

by JoAnn Early Macken

Reading consultant: Susan Nations, M.Ed.,
author/literacy coach/consultant in literacy development

Please visit our web site at: www.earlyliteracy.cc
For a free color catalog describing Weekly Reader® Early Learning Library's
list of high-quality books, call 1-877-445-5824 (USA) or 1-800-387-3178 (Canada).
Weekly Reader® Early Learning Library's fax: (414) 336-0164.

Library of Congress Cataloging-in-Publication Data

Macken, JoAnn Early, 1953-
    The life cycle of a dragonfly / by JoAnn Early Macken.
        p. cm. — (Things with wings)
    Includes index.
    ISBN 0-8368-6381-X (lib. bdg.)
    ISBN 0-8368-6388-7 (softcover)
    1. Dragonflies—Life cycles—Juvenile literature.   I. Title.
    QL520.M33   2006
    595.7'33—dc22   2005026541

This edition first published in 2006 by
Weekly Reader® Early Learning Library
A Member of the WRC Media Family of Companies
330 West Olive Street, Suite 100
Milwaukee, WI 53212 USA

Copyright © 2006 by Weekly Reader® Early Learning Library

Managing editor: Dorothy L. Gibbs
Art direction: Tammy West
Photo research: Diane Laska-Swanke

Photo credits: Cover, © John Gerlach/Visuals Unlimited; p. 5 © Duncan McEwan/naturepl.com;
p. 7 © Rolf Nussbaumer/naturepl.com; p. 9 © Gary Meszaros/Visuals Unlimited; pp. 11, 17, 21
© Richard Day/Daybreak Imagery; pp. 13, 19 © James P. Rowan; p. 15 © Martin Dohrn/naturepl.com

Printed in the United States of America

1 2 3 4 5 6 7 8 9 10 09 08 07 06

Note to Educators and Parents

Reading is such an exciting adventure for young children! They are beginning to integrate their oral language skills with written language. To encourage children along the path to early literacy, books must be colorful, engaging, and interesting; they should invite the young reader to explore both the print and the pictures.

Things with Wings is a new series designed to help children read about fascinating animals, all of which have wings. In each book, young readers will learn about the life cycle of the featured animal, as well as other interesting facts.

Each book is specially designed to support the young reader in the reading process. The familiar topics are appealing to young children and invite them to read — and re-read — again and again. The full-color photographs and enhanced text further support the student during the reading process.

In addition to serving as wonderful picture books in schools, libraries, homes, and other places where children learn to love reading, these books are specifically intended to be read within an instructional guided reading group. This small group setting allows beginning readers to work with a fluent adult model as they make meaning from the text. After children develop fluency with the text and content, the book can be read independently. Children and adults alike will find these books supportive, engaging, and fun!

— Susan Nations, M.Ed., author, literacy coach,
and consultant in literacy development

Dragonfly eggs hatch in water. The young dragonflies, called **nymphs**, live in the water. They eat the nymphs of other insects.

dragonfly
nymph

A dragonfly nymph **molts**, or sheds its skin, many times as it grows. When it is fully grown, it climbs out of the water. Then it molts one last time.

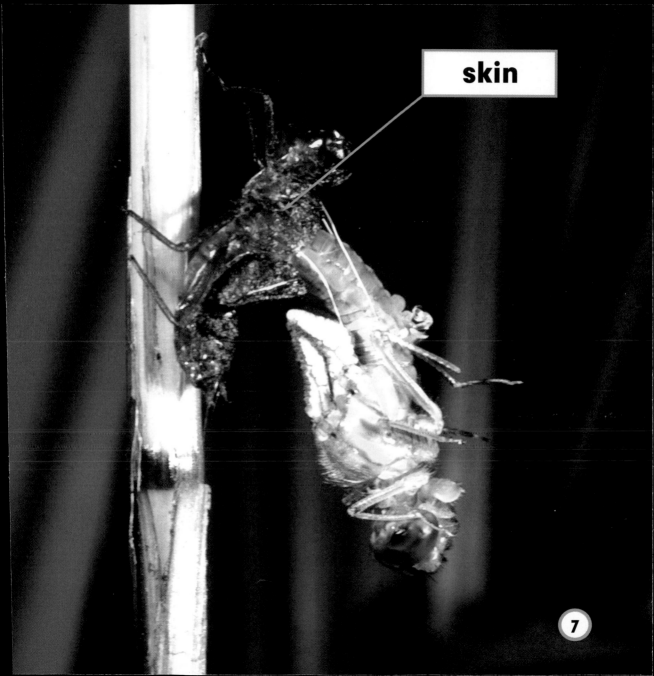

skin

7

Adult dragonflies have four shiny wings. The wings on some dragonflies are as clear as windows. Others have spots of color.

Dragonflies have long, thin bodies. Many kinds are brightly colored. Like all insects, they have six legs.

Dragonflies have huge eyes. They can turn their heads to see all around them. They watch out for birds and spiders.

eyes

13

Most dragonflies live near water. They are strong, fast fliers. They may fly many miles to find food.

Dragonflies catch their food as they fly. Mosquitoes are their main food. Flies, wasps, and moths are also their prey.

moth

Most dragonflies fly when the sun shines. When the sky is cloudy, they hide. They rest on leaves or rocks.

Most dragonflies live only a few weeks. In that short time, they change color. Female dragonflies lay their eggs in the water. Later, new nymphs hatch.

The Life Cycle of a Dragonfly

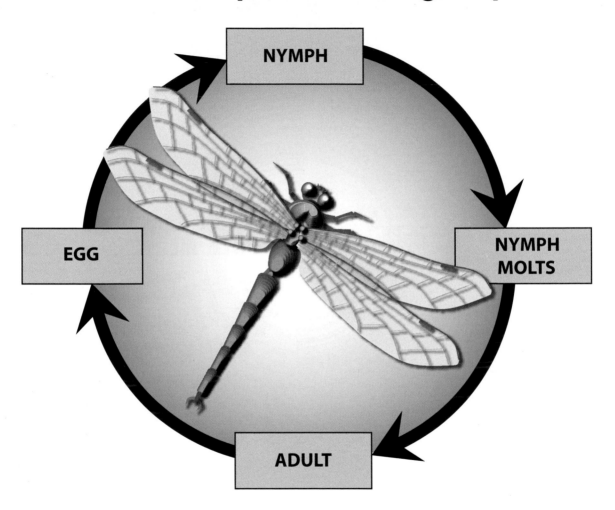

NYMPH

EGG

NYMPH MOLTS

ADULT

Glossary

hatch — to break out of an egg

molts — sheds, or loses, the skin

mosquitoes — small flying insects that bite

nymphs — young insects

prey — an animal that is hunted for food

Index

About the Author

JoAnn Early Macken is the author of two rhyming picture books, *Sing-Along Song* and *Cats on Judy*, and more than eighty nonfiction books for children. Her poems have appeared in several children's magazines. A graduate of the M.F.A. in Writing for Children and Young Adults Program at Vermont College, she lives in Wisconsin with her husband and their two sons.